Twenty to Make

Bunting and Pennants

Kate Haxell

Search Press

First published in Great Britain 2011

Search Press Limited
Wellwood, North Farm Road,
Tunbridge Wells, Kent TN2 3DR

Reprinted 2011, 2012, 2013

Photographs by Paul Bricknell and
Debbie Patterson at Search Press Studios and
on location

Print ISBN: 978-1-84448-698-4
Epub ISBN: 978-1-78126-038-8
Mobi ISBN: 978-1-78126-093-7
PDF ISBN: 978-1-78126-147-7

Suppliers
If you have difficulty in obtaining any of the materials and equipment mentioned in this book, then please visit the Search Press website for details of suppliers: www.searchpress.com

Printed in Malaysia

Many thanks to Rebecca Clibbens for the use of her beautiful home for the photography in this book.

Contents

Introduction

Long established as decoration for outdoor parties and events, bunting has a wonderful retro charm that is perfectly in tune with today's fashion for the vintage look. No longer confined to the outdoors – and no longer needing to be miles in length – you can revel in bunting as seasonal and year-round decoration in any room in the house. Making your own allows you to use fabrics and trimmings that perfectly complement your room schemes. Best of all, bunting is quick and easy to make and is a great way of using up scraps from your fabric stash. You could also make the pennants and flags from the projects separately for individual decorations.

In this book you'll find twenty bunting projects ranging from traditional pennants in shabby chic fabrics, to winter wonderland snowflakes, to breezy seaside-style flags. If you are looking for something sophisticated for an adult's room, something quirky for a teenager, or something sweet for a baby, there's a project here for you. If you like to whizz up a project on the sewing machine then you'll find lots to choose from, but if you prefer some hand-sewing in front of a good film, then you won't be disappointed in the range of ideas on offer. And whether you live in a colourful, boho house or a marvellously serene apartment, a beach house or a modern home, there are projects that will suit you and your style. Bunting really is for everyone.

All the designs are easy to make and some are super-speedy, too. The more elaborate designs will be effective in short lengths: five sparkling butterflies are all you need to create a statement in a girl's room. You can even make up one individual pennant, and hang it singly on some ribbon or cord for a subtle but stylish look in any room. You need no special skills and all necessary templates are given on each project's page. So there's no excuse not to make a string of fabulous bunting this afternoon.

Techniques

Other than simple machine- and hand-sewing, the only techniques you need to know to make your own bunting are how to use the templates and how to clip curves, corners and points so that your flags and pennants lie flat.

Blanket stitch

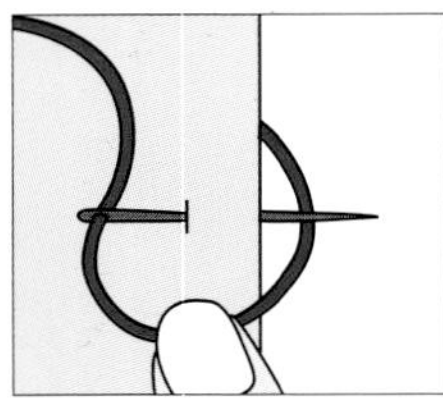

1 Secure the thread on the back of the fabric. From the front, slip the needle through the fabric on the stitching line. Loop the working thread under the point of the needle.

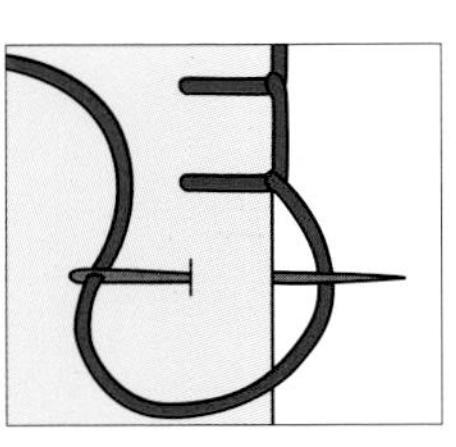

2 Carefully pull the needle through and tighten the stitch. Continue working stitches in this way, tightening each one so that a strand of thread lies along the edge of the fabric.

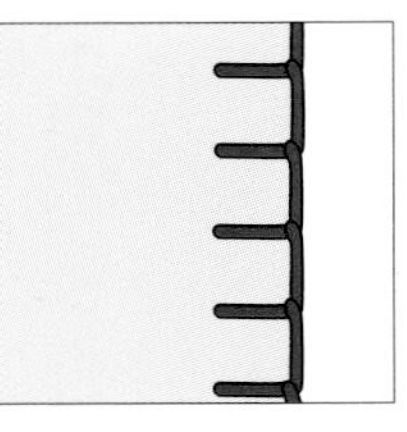

3 Space the stitches evenly for a neat finish. To avoid distorting stitches or puckering fabric, pull the threads gently.

Chain stitch

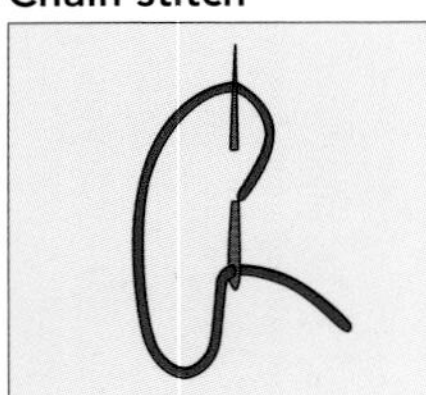

1 Bring the needle through the fabric to the start of the sewing line. Take the needle back down very close to where it came up, then bring it back up to the surface at the end position of the first stitch. Loop the thread under the point of the needle and pull through. Adjust the stitch to make a neat loop.

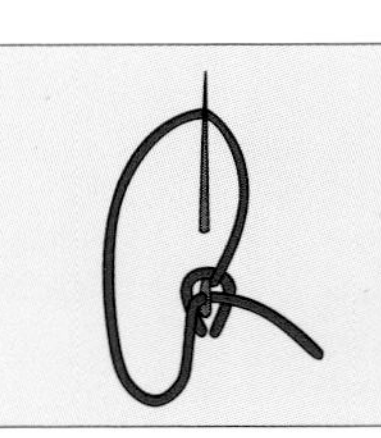

2 Take the needle back down close to where it came up in the loop and bring it up at the end position of the next stitch. Loop the thread under the point of the needle and pull through.

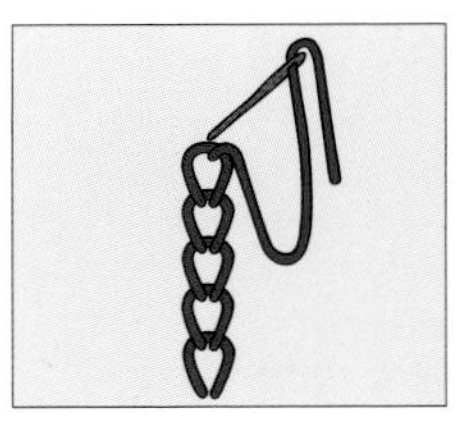

3 Continue to create a chain of links and finish by catching the final loop with a small stitch to avoid the chain coming undone.

Stab stitch

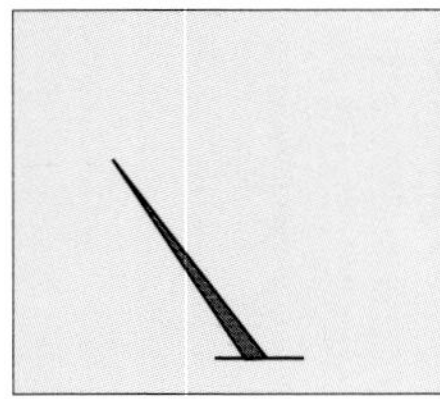

1 Secure the thread and bring the needle up from the back of the fabric.

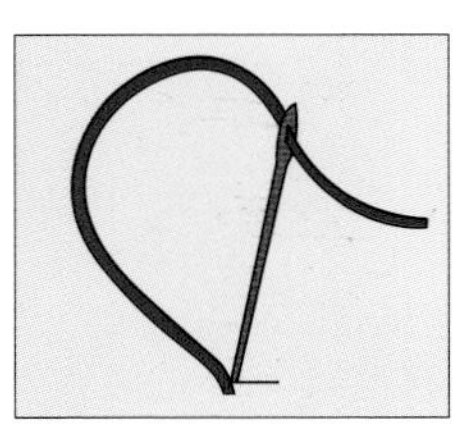

2 'Stab' the needle straight back down very close to where you brought it up. Draw the thread through to make a small stitch, then repeat to create stitches close to each other or as instructed.

Slip stitch

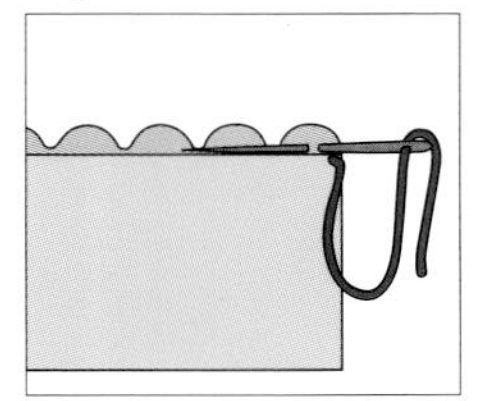

1 Secure the end of the thread on the back of the fabric. Take the needle through just a couple of threads on the back of the ric-rac.

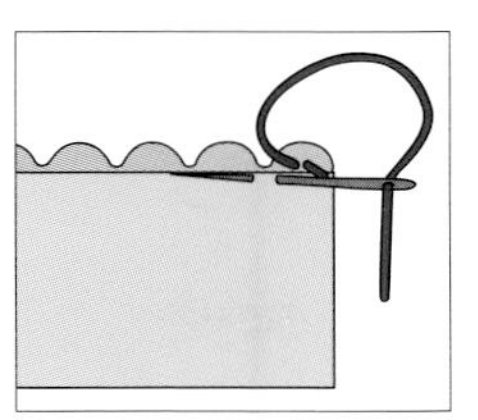

2 Pull the sewing thread through, then take the needle through the fabric, again picking up just a couple of threads.

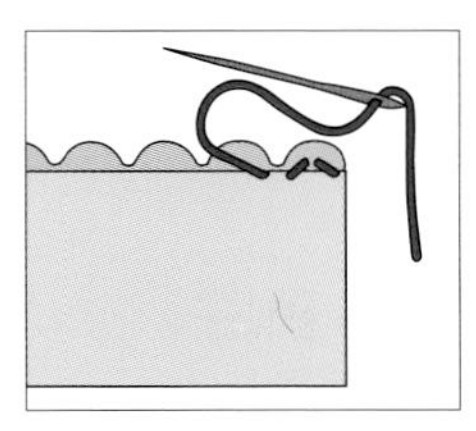

3 As you work along the row of stitches in this way, pull the thread gently to keep the stitches taut. Don't pull too hard or you will pucker the fabric.

Using the templates

You will find each template on the project's page where required. Other than the three snowflake motifs, all the motifs given are symmetrical and only half the shape is shown. To make a full template, enlarge the motif on a photocopier by the amount stated in the project. Fold the paper down the dotted line then cut out the shape, cutting through both layers of paper.

Stitching and clipping points

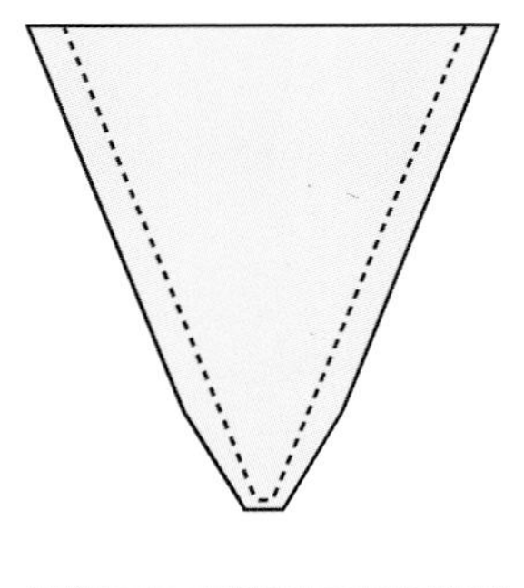

Sew down one side of the pennant, stopping just before you reach the stitching line for the other side. (If you find it hard to judge the position of this stitching line, measure and mark it with a fabric marker before you start sewing.) Lift the presser foot and turn the fabric so that the foot is parallel to the top edge. Turn the hand wheel on the machine to make a single stitch, which should bring you to the second stitching line. Lift the presser foot again and turn the fabric to sew the second side of the pennant.

Trim the point off the pennant just below the stitching. Cut away some fabric from the seam allowances either side of the point.

Clipping corners

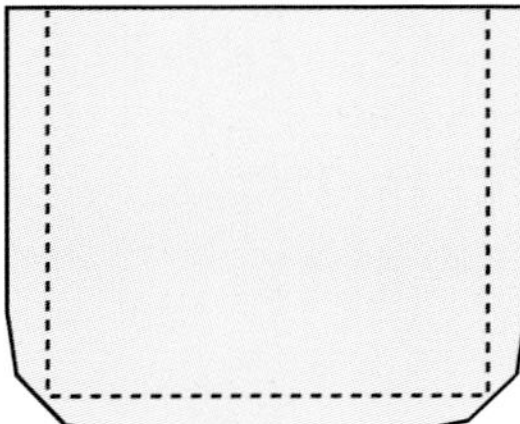

Trim the corner off the flag just beyond the stitching. Cut away some fabric from the seam allowances either side of the corner.

Clipping curves

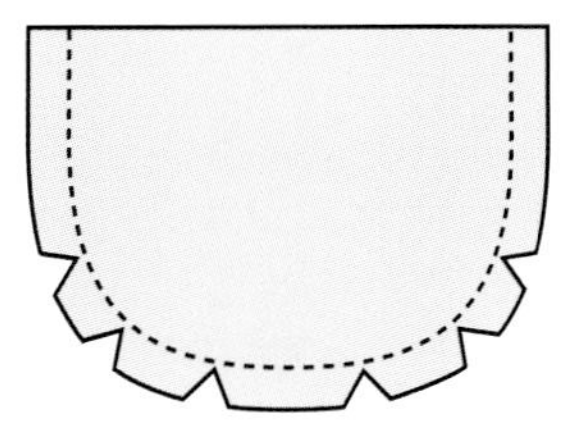

Cut small wedges out of the seam allowances, cutting up close to the stitching. Space the wedges quite close together on tighter curves and further apart on softer ones.

Almost Instant Bunting

Materials:

Card for template

For each pennant: piece of cotton fabric measuring at least 9 x 13cm (3½ x 5in)

2.5cm (1in) bias binding the required length of the bunting, allowing for ties at each end

Sewing thread to match bias binding

Tools:

Pencil

Ruler

Paper scissors

Spray starch

Iron

Fabric marker

Rotary cutter with pinking wheel or pinking shears

Cutting mat (if using rotary cutter)

Pins

Sewing machine

Instructions:

1 On the card, draw a triangle 8cm (3¼in) wide across the top and 12cm (4¾in) from top to tip. Cut this out to make a template.

2 Starch the pieces of fabric, following the manufacturer's instructions. Use the template and fabric marker to draw as many pennants as you need on to the fabrics. Cut them out using the rotary cutter and mat or a pair of pinking shears.

3 Press the binding in half lengthways. Slip the top edge of each pennant into the binding, spacing the pennants evenly. Pin each one in place. Turn under and pin the ends of the binding to neaten them.

4 Set the sewing machine to a narrow zigzag. Starting at one end of the binding, machine along it close to the open edge, sewing over each pennant and taking out the pins as you go. Press the bunting.

Tip: cutting pinked edges
If you are using pinking shears, it's worth taking the time to match up the zigzag pattern along the edges of the pennants for the best finish. Make the first cut, then open the blades and line up the pattern in the edge of the fabric with the serrations in the blades before making the next cut. If you are using a rotary cutter, then cut each edge in one stroke to keep the pattern regular.

Raid your stash bag, recycle old garments, make full use of inexpensive remnants and whip up lots of this easy-to-make bunting to decorate your home for a party. Starching the fabric gives the bunting a crisp finish but isn't vital, so you can skip that stage if you are in a hurry.

Mini Bunting

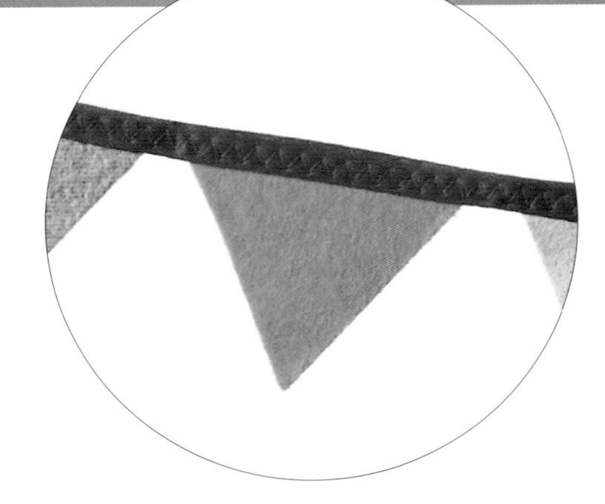

Materials:

Card for template

For each pennant: piece of felt measuring at least 5 x 5cm (2 x 2in)

1.5cm (5/8in) bias binding the required length of the bunting, allowing for ties at each end

Sewing thread to match bias binding

Tools:

Paper scissors

Fabric marker

Ruler

Rotary cutter or fabric scissors

Cutting mat (if using rotary cutter)

Iron

Pins

Sewing machine

Instructions:

1 On the card, draw a triangle 5cm (2in) wide across the top and 4.5cm (1¾in) from top to tip. Cut this out to make a template. Use the template and fabric marker to draw as many pennants as you need on to felt. Cut them out using the rotary cutter and mat or a pair of scissors.

2 Iron the binding in half. Slip the top edge of each pennant into the binding, spacing the pennants evenly. Pin each one in place.

3 Set the sewing machine to a narrow zigzag. Starting at one end of the binding, machine along it close to the open edge, sewing over each pennant and taking out the pins as you go. Press the bunting.

Quick and easy to make, this bunting is perfect for trimming a shelf in the playroom. It's also the right scale for children to use in games with their bears and dolls.

Beach Bunting

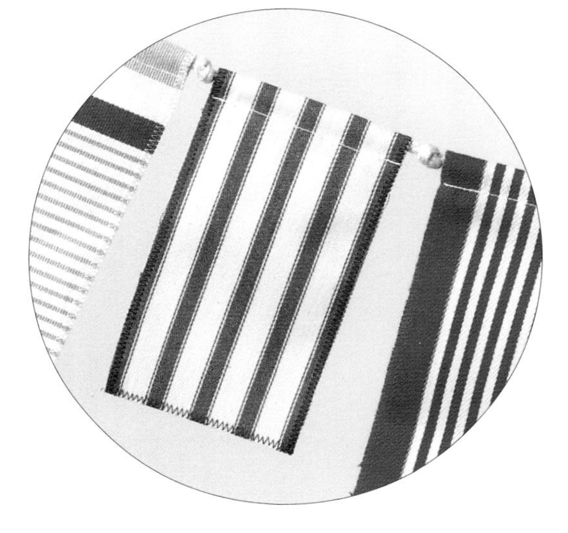

Materials:

For each flag: piece of ticking fabric measuring the required width by the required height plus 2cm (¾in)

Sewing threads to match fabrics

Cotton cord the required length of the bunting, allowing for ties at each end, plus 2cm (¾in) for each knot

Tools:

Fabric scissors

Ruler

Sewing machine

Iron

Pins

Instructions:

1 Set the sewing machine to a narrow zigzag stitch. Zigzag right around the edge of each piece of fabric. Press the flags.

2 Turn under and pin 2cm (¾in) at the top of each flag. Set the sewing machine to a medium straight stitch and hem the turn-under, sewing close to the edge and taking out the pins as you go.

3 Thread the flags on to the cord, tying a knot between each flag to hold it in place, plus a knot at either end of the cord.

Tip: neat corners
To make neat zigzag corners, stop sewing at the end of one side of the fabric with the needle to the right. Lift the presser foot and turn the fabric 90 degrees. Start sewing the next side of the fabric.

This ticking bunting will add sunny seaside appeal to any room. Practise the zigzag stitch on a scrap of fabric to check the stitch width, and perfect the corner-turning technique before you start your flags.

Flower Power Bunting

Materials:

Card for template

For each pennant: two pieces of floral cotton fabric measuring at least 17 x 20cm (6¾ x 8in)

Sewing thread

2cm (¾in) floral bias binding the required length of the bunting, allowing for ties at each end

Tools:

Pencil

Ruler

Paper scissors

Fabric marker

Fabric scissors

Pins

Sewing machine

Iron

Instructions:

1 On the card draw a triangle 17cm (6¾in) wide across the top and 20cm (8in) from top to tip. Cut this out to make a template. Use the template and fabric marker to draw as many pennants as you need on to the fabric. Cut out each one and pin them together in pairs, right sides together, matching all edges.

2 Set the sewing machine to a medium straight stitch. Taking a 1cm (3/8in) seam allowance, machine-sew down both sloping sides of each pennant (see page 7), leaving the straight top edge open.

3 Trim the seam allowances and clip the point of each pennant (see page 7). Turn each pennant right side out and press flat. You will find the end of a knitting needle useful for turning out the point, but be careful not to push the needle right through the fabric.

4 Set the sewing machine to a medium zigzag stitch. Sew across the top of each pennant to stiffen the edge and prevent it from fraying.

5 Slip the top edge of each pennant into the binding, spacing the pennants evenly. Pin each one in place. Turn under and pin the ends of the binding to neaten them.

6 Set the sewing machine to a medium straight stitch. Starting at one end of the binding, machine along it close to the open edge, sewing over each pennant and taking out the pins as you go. Press the bunting.

Summer flowers come indoors with this colourful bunting. Choose contrasting and complementary floral designs for a burst of colour, whatever the weather outdoors.

Pom-Pom Bunting

Materials:

Card for template

For each pennant: two pieces of fabric measuring at least 17 x 18cm (6¾ x 7in)

Pom-pom trims

Sewing thread

Individual pom-poms

Strip of straight-grain fabric (or several joined strips) measuring 5cm (2in) by the required length of the bunting, allowing for ties at each end

Tools:

Pencil

Ruler

Paper scissors

Fabric marker

Fabric scissors

Pins

Sewing machine

Iron

3cm (1¼in) bias tape maker

Hand-sewing needle

Instructions:

1 On the card draw a triangle 17cm (6¾in) wide across the top and 18cm (7in) from top to tip. Cut this out to make a template. Use the template and fabric marker to draw as many pennants as you need on to the fabric. Cut out each one. To make untrimmed pennants, follow steps 1–4 of Flower Power Bunting (see page 14). Hand-sew individual pom-poms to the points of these pennants.

2 To make trimmed pennants, pin the pom-pom trim to the right side of one pennant piece. Position it with the braid edge less than 1cm (3/8in) in from the raw edge of the fabric, so that when the pennant is sewn with a 1cm (3/8in) seam allowance, only the pom-poms – no braid – will show. Tack the braid in place, then pin the other pennant piece on top, right sides together, matching all edges.

3 Set the sewing machine to a medium straight stitch and fit a zip foot. Taking a 1cm (3/8in) seam allowance, machine-sew down both sloping sides of each pennant (see page 7), leaving the straight top edge open.

4 Trim the seam allowances and clip the point of each pennant (see page 7). Turn each pennant right side out and press flat, being careful not to press the bobbles. You will find the end of a knitting needle useful for turning out the point, but be careful not to push the needle right through the fabric. Set the sewing machine to a medium zigzag stitch and sew across the top of each pennant.

5 Following the manufacturer's instructions, thread the strip of straight-grain fabric through the tape maker and iron the folds into tape as they emerge. Press the tape in half lengthways.

6 Slip the top edge of each pennant into the binding, spacing the pennants evenly. Pin each one in place. Cut very short pieces of braid with a single pom-pom on from the trim and slip them into the binding between some pennants. Pin them in place. Turn under and pin the ends of the binding to neaten them.

7 Set the sewing machine to a medium straight stitch. Starting at one end of the binding, machine along it close to the open edge, sewing over each pennant and piece of pom-pom braid and taking out the pins as you go. Press the bunting.

Tip: making tape
It's better to cut strips of fabric to go through a tape maker than it is to tear them. The rippled edges of torn fabric tend to run unevenly through the maker, producing tape that varies in width.

Jaunty spotted pennants with pom-pom trim look fun in a playroom or child's bedroom. For a more sophisticated look, collect different spotty fabrics in one colour palette and make the bunting from those.

Wild West Bunting

Materials:

Card for template

For each printed pennant: piece of Wild West print and piece of gingham fabric measuring at least 14 x 15cm (5½ x 6in)

For each check pennant: two pieces of gingham fabric measuring at least 14 x 15cm (5½ x 6in)

Sewing thread

Cotton cord the required length of the bunting, allowing for ties at each end

Tools:

Pencil

Ruler

Craft knife

Cutting mat

Fabric marker

Fabric scissors

Pins

Sewing machine

Hand-sewing needle

Instructions:

1 On the card draw a triangle 13cm (5in) wide across the top and 14.5cm (5¾in) from top to tip. Using the craft knife and cutting mat, cut out the triangle, being careful not to cut into the surrounding card. Remove the triangle and use the frame you have made to position the pennants to best effect on the printed fabric. Using the fabric marker, draw around the inside of the frame to make as many pennants as required. Repeat the process on the gingham fabric to make backs for these pennants, and to make the fronts and backs of the gingham pennants.

2 Pin the front and back of each pennant together, right sides together, matching all edges. Set the sewing machine to a medium straight stitch. Using the edge of the foot as a guide, sew across the straight top edge of a pennant. Starting 1.5cm (5/8in) down from this top line of sewing, and again using the edge of the foot as a guide, sew down to the point of the pennant, turn (see page 7), and sew up the other edge, stopping 1.5cm (5/8in) from the top line.

3 Clip the point of the pennant (see page 7) and turn it right side out through one of the gaps in the top corners. Tuck in these corners, clipping off any excess fabric if necessary. Press the pennant. Repeat the process to make up all the pennants.

4 Thread all the pennants on to the cord, passing the cord through the gaps in the top corners of each pennant.

5 Space the pennants evenly along the cord. Using the sewing needle and thread, make a little stitch through the back of each pennant and into the cord to hold it in place.

6 Tie a knot in each end of the cord.

This is perfect playroom bunting and you can choose a printed fabric in a colourway and theme to complement your child's room and interests. Intersperse the printed pennants with plainer ones (gingham is used here) to stop the bunting looking too busy.

Christmas Tree Bunting

Materials:

Paper for template

For each tree: two pieces of fabric measuring at least 14 x 11cm (5½ x 4½in)

Fusible webbing

Beading thread

Selection of sequins of different sizes in one colour

Seed beads

2.5cm (1in) ribbon the required length of the bunting, allowing for ties at each end

Tools:

Pencil

Paper scissors

Iron

Fabric scissors

Beading needle

Instructions:

1 Enlarge the tree motif and cut it out to make a template. Draw around it on to the paper backing of the webbing once for every tree required.

2 Roughly cut out the shapes and, following the manufacturer's instructions, iron them on to the wrong side of the fabrics that will be the tree fronts. Cut out the trees accurately. Peel off the paper backing and iron the trees on to the wrong side of the tree back fabrics. Carefully cut around the front shapes to cut out each tree.

3 Using the beading needle and thread, decorate each tree with sequins. Bring the needle up where you want the sequin to be, slip one or more sequins on to the needle, topped by a seed bead. Skipping the bead, take the needle down through the sequins and fabric. Make a tiny stitch at the back to hold the sequin in place, then slide the needle between the layers of fabric to the position of the next sequin (this avoids having long threads on the back of the tree).

4 Sew the top of each tree to the ribbon, spacing them evenly. Sew on a sequin and bead (I used snowflake sequins) to cover the stitching.

5 Turn under and hem the ends of the ribbon to neaten them.

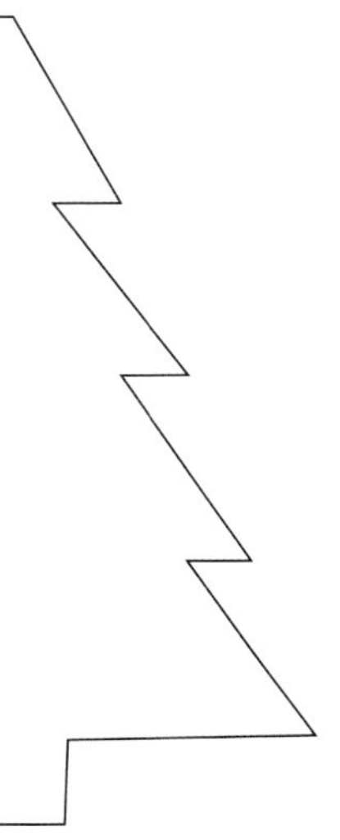

The template shown half of actual size. Enlarge 200% on a photocopier.

Tip: choosing fabrics

Make the most of scraps of decorative fabric by using them just for the tree fronts and make the backs from plain fabric: I used a medium-weight wool to give the trees a bit of substance.

This isn't the quickest bunting to make, but it's not at all difficult and you can do most of it on your lap in front of the television. Make one tree a night in the run-up to Christmas and you'll have a gorgeous decoration for your home.

Name Bunting

Materials:

Letters enlarged to fit in 8 x 5cm (3 x 2in) rectangle

Piece of cotton fabric measuring at least 8 x 5cm (3 x 2in) for each letter

Fusible webbing

For each flag: two pieces of cotton fabric measuring at least 12 x 9cm (4¾ x 3½in)

Stranded embroidery thread

Sewing thread

1.5cm (5/8in) bias binding the required length of the bunting, allowing for ties at each end

Decorative buttons

Tools:

Paper scissors

Iron

Fabric marker

Ruler

Hand-sewing needle

Embroidery needle

Fabric scissors

Pins

Sewing machine

Instructions:

1 Cut out the letters to make templates. You can photocopy letters from a copyright-free book or print out the required name at the right size in your choice of font. Iron the fusible webbing onto the wrong side of the letter fabric. Lay the letters the wrong way around on the paper backing of the webbing and draw around them. Cut out the fabric letters.

2 Cut out 12 x 9cm (4¾ x 3½in) rectangles from the flag fabrics. Peel the paper backing off each letter. Position the letters centrally in the rectangles and iron them in place. Using the embroidery needle and two strands of embroidery thread, work decorative blanket stitch around the edges of each letter.

3 Pin the front and back of each flag together, right sides together, matching all edges. Set the sewing machine to a medium straight stitch. Taking a 1cm (3/8in) seam allowance, sew down one side, across the bottom and up the other side of each flag, leaving the top edge open. As you sew the corners, round them off with the line of stitching. Clip the seam allowances (see page 7) and turn the flags right side out.

4 Iron the bias binding in half. Slip the top edge of each flag into the binding, spacing the flags evenly. Pin each one in place.

5 Set the sewing machine to a narrow zigzag. Starting at one end of the binding, machine along it close to the open edge. Sew over each flag, taking out the pins as you go. Press the bunting.

6 Sew the buttons on to the bunting to best effect.

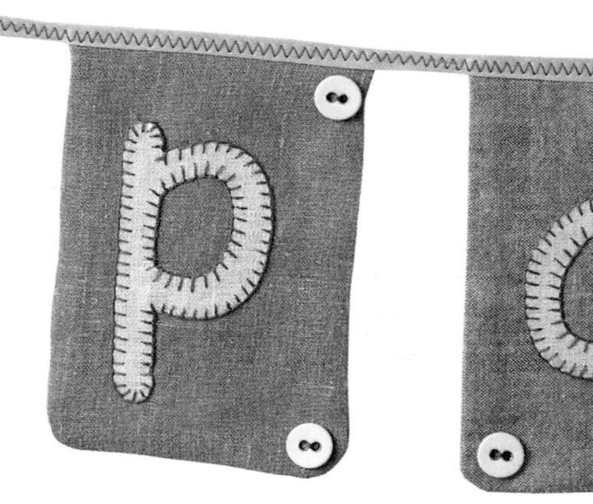

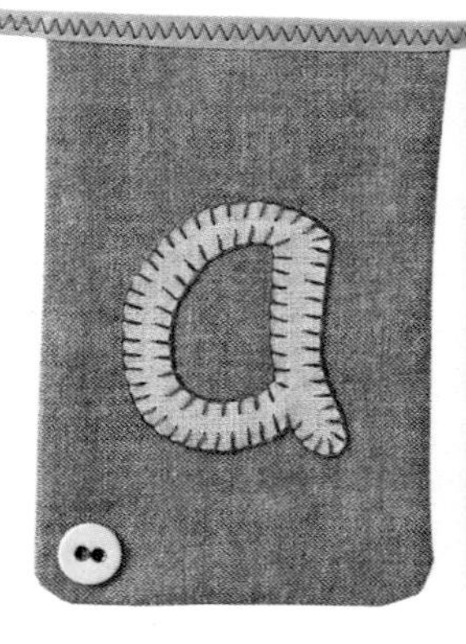

This cute bunting makes a great welcome for a new baby, though don't expect it to get set aside as your child grows up. Use the same principles to make 'Merry Christmas' or 'Happy Birthday' bunting.

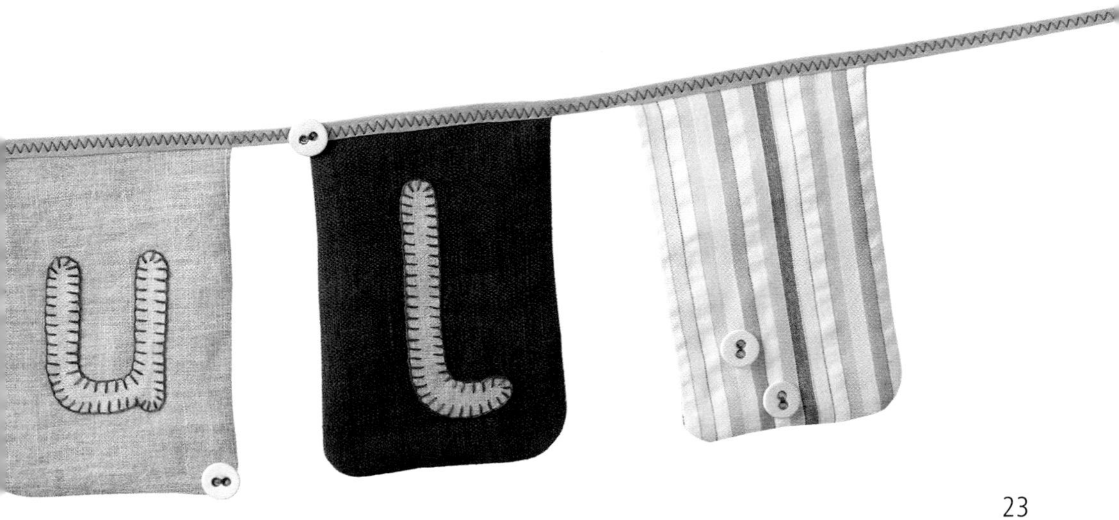

Scalloped Bunting

Materials:

Paper for template

For each scallop: two pieces of fabric measuring at least 12 x 10cm (4¾ x 4in)

Sewing thread

Narrow ric-rac in colours to tone with fabrics

Strip of straight-grain fabric (or several joined strips) measuring 5cm (2in) by the required length of the bunting, allowing for ties at each end

Tools:

Paper scissors

Fabric marker

Iron

Pins

Sewing machine

Hand-sewing needle

3cm (1¼in) bias tape maker

Instructions:

1 Enlarge the scallop motif and cut it out to make a template. Use the template and fabric marker to draw as many scallops as you need on to the fabric. Cut out each one and pin them together in pairs, right sides together, matching all edges.

2 Set the sewing machine to a small straight stitch. Keeping the edge of the presser foot against the edge of the fabric, sew around the curve on each flag. Leave the straight (top) edge open. Take out the pins.

3 Press each flag, clip the curves (see page 7) and turn right side out. Press each scallop flat, pressing the seam carefully to get a smooth curve.

4 Using the hand-sewing needle and thread and working from the back so that the stitches don't show, slip stitch a length of narrow ric-rac to the front of each scallop, around the curved edge.

5 Following the manufacturer's instructions, thread the strip of straight-grain fabric through the tape maker and iron the folds into tape as they emerge. Press the tape in half lengthways.

6 Slip the top edge of each scallop into the binding, spacing the scallops evenly. Pin each one in place. Turn under and pin the ends of the binding to neaten them.

7 Set the sewing machine to a medium zigzag stitch. Starting at one end of the binding, machine along it close to the open edge, sewing over each scallop and taking out the pins as you go. Press the bunting.

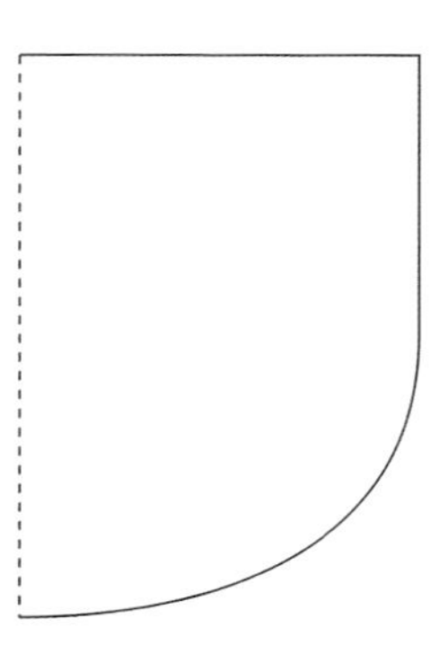

The template shown half of actual size. Enlarge 200% on a photocopier.

A pretty, vintage-style bunting that has lots of charm. The ric-rac edging is a lovely touch, but if you aren't keen on hand-sewing you can leave it off and your bunting will still look lovely.

Wedding Bunting

Materials:

Card for template

For each pennant: piece of fabric measuring at least 12 x 15cm (4¾ x 6in)

2.5cm (1in) organza ribbon the required length of the bunting, allowing for ties at each end

Beading thread

Seed beads

Tools:

Pencil

Ruler

Paper scissors

Fabric marker

Rotary cutter with pinking wheel or pinking shears

Cutting mat (if using rotary cutter)

Pins

Sewing machine

Iron

Beading needle

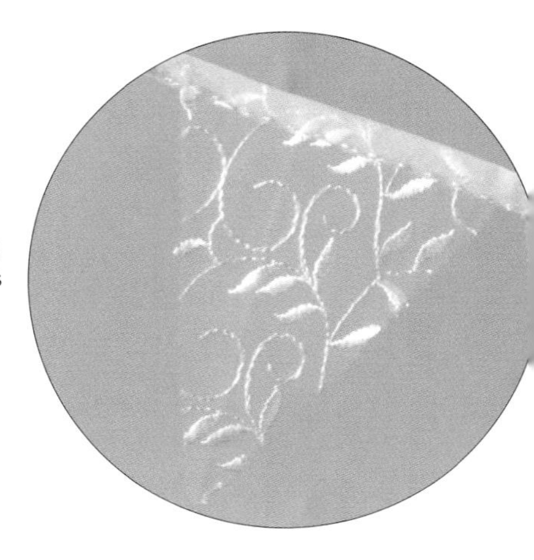

Instructions:

1 On the card draw a triangle 12cm (4¾in) wide across the top and 15cm (6in) from top to tip. Cut this out to make a template. Use the template and fabric marker to draw as many pennants as you need on to the fabric. Cut out each one using a rotary cutter with a pinking wheel or a pair of pinking shears.

2 Press the ribbon in half lengthways. Slip the top edge of each pennant into the ribbon, butting the corner of one against the corner of the next. Pin each one in place. Turn under and pin the ends of the ribbon to neaten them.

3 Thread the beading needle with a long length of beading thread. Starting at one end, first stitch the end of the ribbon in place. Then work a line of running stitch along the open edges of the ribbon, very close to the edges, sewing them together. Thread on a seed bead with each stitch. At the edges of each pennant, make a backstitch through a bead to stop the running stitch being able to gather up.

You could decorate a wedding venue with this bunting, made in fabrics to match the wedding colour theme. For a speedier version, replace the organza ribbon with bias binding and machine-sew the pennants to it as for Almost Instant Bunting, see page 8.

Pleated Fan Bunting

Materials:

For each fan: piece of fabric measuring 30 x 10cm (12 x 4in)

Fusible hemming tape

Sewing thread

1.5cm (5/8in) bias binding the required length of the bunting, allowing for ties at each end

Two decorative buttons for each fan, plus one more

Tools:

Fabric scissors

Ruler

Iron

Hand-sewing needle

Sewing machine

Instructions:

1 Press under a 1cm (3/8in) hem on each edge of a piece of fabric. Following the manufacturer's instructions, use the fusible hemming tape to hem one long edge; this will be the lower edge of the fan. (Using the tape helps to stiffen the edge and so is better than sewing a hem.)

2 Thread the hand-sewing needle and double the thread. Knot the end of the thread to secure it, and working very close to the top edge of the strip of fabric, sew a line of 1cm (3/8in) running stitches. Start the stitching with the needle going in from the front and end it with the needle coming through from the back; this will make the edges of the first and last pleats face neatly to the back. Pull the stitches up very tightly to form a fabric fan. Make a securing backstitch, then sew the inner edge of the top pleats on either side together at the centre to hold the fan shape.

3 Set the sewing machine to a medium zigzag stitch. Fold the bias binding in half and turn under and pin the ends to neaten them. Starting at one end of the binding, zigzag stitch right along it.

4 Hand-sew the centre of the first fan to the binding, then stretch out the fan and sew the tip of each end to the binding. Sew on the next fan so that the tip touches the one just sewn on: no binding should be visible. Continue sewing on all the fans.

5 Sew a button over the gathered centre of each fan and one over each pair of joined tips.

This is a fresh twist on a style of bunting very popular in the United States. I have used the red, white and blue theme of Independence Day, but you can, of course, choose any colours you like.

Valentine Bunting

Materials:

Paper for template

For each heart: piece of felt measuring at least 7 x 6cm (2¾ x 2½in)

Seed beads

Sewing thread

1.5cm (5/8in) ric-rac the required length of the bunting, allowing for ties at each end

Tools:

Paper scissors

Fabric marker

Beading needle

Fabric scissors

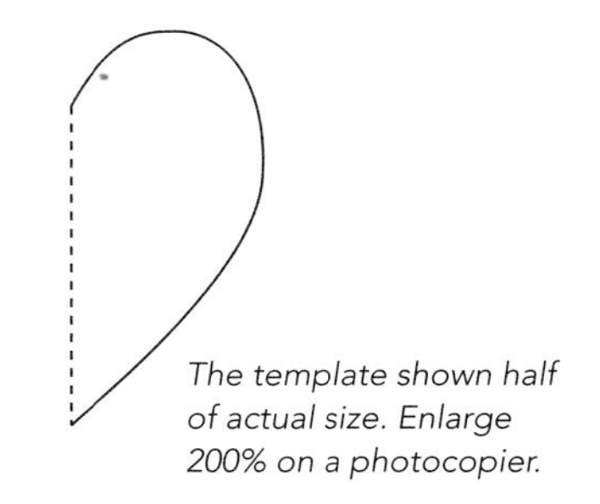

The template shown half of actual size. Enlarge 200% on a photocopier.

Instructions:

1 Enlarge the heart motif and cut it out to make a template.

2 Using the fabric marker, draw around the template on to the felt and cut out as many hearts as needed.

3 Using the beading needle, sewing thread and seed beads, edge each heart with beaded blanket stitch (see page 6). Slip a bead on to the needle, from front to back take a tiny stitch through the edge of the felt and work blanket stitch in the usual way, but push the bead as far up the thread as possible so that as you tighten the stitch, the bead lies on the edge of the heart. This may sound fiddly, but once you get into the rhythm of the stitch you'll be pleasantly surprised at how quickly you work around a heart.

4 Using individual stab stitches, with one bead on each stitch and following the photograph for guidance, work a simple design in beads on each heart.

5 Using tiny stab stitches through the edge of the felt and stitching through the appropriate beads, sew the top of each heart lobe to the edge of the ric-rac, spacing the hearts evenly.

6 Turn under and sew the ends of the ric-rac to neaten them.

A mini-bunting with a Scandinavian feel, these sweetly romantic hearts are deceptively intricate looking; they are actually very easy to make. Only hand-sewing is needed, so while this isn't the quickest bunting to make, it's a perfect lap project for working in front of the television. A variation in white would make a charming wedding decoration.

Spots & Stripes Bunting

Materials:

Card for template

For each pennant: two pieces of fabric measuring at least 15 x 15cm (6 x 6in)

For each flag: two pieces of fabric measuring at least 10 x 20cm (4 x 8in)

Sewing thread

4cm (1½in) ribbon the required length of the bunting, allowing for ties at each end

Tools:

Pencil

Ruler

Paper scissors

Fabric marker

Fabric scissors

Pins

Sewing machine

Iron

Instructions:

1 On the card draw a triangle 15cm (6in) wide across the top and 15cm (6in) from top to tip. Cut this out to make a template. Use the template and fabric marker to draw as many pennants as you need on to the fabric. Cut out each one and pin them together in pairs, right sides together, matching all the edges.

2 Using the fabric marker, draw as many 10 x 20cm (4 x 8in) flags as you need on to the fabric. Cut each one out and pin them together in pairs, right sides together, matching all the edges.

3 Set the sewing machine to a medium straight stitch. Taking a 1cm (3/8in) seam allowance, machine-sew down both sloping sides of each pennant (see page 7), leaving the straight top edge open. Machine down one long edge, across a short edge and up the second long edge of each flag, leaving the top short edge open.

4 Trim the seam allowances and clip the point of each pennant and corners of each flag (see page 7). Turn each pennant and flag right side out and press flat. You will find the end of a knitting needle useful for turning out the points and corners, but be careful not to push the needle right through the fabric.

5 Set the sewing machine to a medium zigzag stitch. Sew across the top of each pennant and flag to stiffen the edge and prevent it from fraying.

6 Fold the ribbon lengthways, so that one edge slightly overlaps the other: the overlapping side will be the front. Press the fold. Placing them alternately, slip the top edge of each pennant and flag into the ribbon, butting the top corners against each other. Turn under and pin the ends of the ribbon to neaten them.

7 Set the sewing machine to a medium straight stitch. Starting at one end of the ribbon, machine along it close to the open edge, sewing over each pennant and flag and taking out the pins as you go. Press the bunting.

I chose just one spotted and one striped fabric for this bunting, but you can make each flag from a different fabric for a very jolly effect. This design also works well with the rectangular flags made from check fabric.

Bells & Tassels Bunting

Materials:

Paper for template

For each flag: two pieces of satin fabric measuring at least 14 x 14cm (5½ x 5½in)

Sewing thread

One small jingle bell for each flag

2.5cm (1in) ribbon the required length of the bunting, allowing for ties at each end

One decorative tassel for every alternate flag

Variegated machine embroidery thread

Tools:

Paper scissors

Fabric marker

Fabric scissors

Pins

Sewing machine

Iron

Hand-sewing needle

Instructions:

1 Enlarge the flag motif and cut it out to make a template. Use the template and fabric marker to draw as many flags as you need on to the fabric. Cut out each one and pin them together in pairs, right sides together, matching all edges.

2 Set the sewing machine to a small straight stitch. Keeping the edge of the presser foot against the edge of the fabric, sew around the curve on each flag. Leave the straight (top) edge open. Take out the pins.

3 Press each flag, clip the curves and point (see page 7) and turn right side out. Press each flag flat, pressing the seam carefully to get smooth curves. Using the hand-sewing needle and sewing thread, sew a small bell to the point of each flag.

4 Fold the ribbon lengthways, so that one edge slightly overlaps the other: the overlapping side will be the front. Press the fold. Trim the hanging strands on each tassel to 1cm (3/8in). Space the flags and tassels so that there is a 2cm (¾in) gap between flags and the same gap between a flag and a tassel, and slip the top edge of each flag and the top of each tassel into the ribbon, pinning them in place. Tack the tassel loops and the flags in place if you are using satin fabrics. Turn under and pin the ends of the ribbon to neaten them.

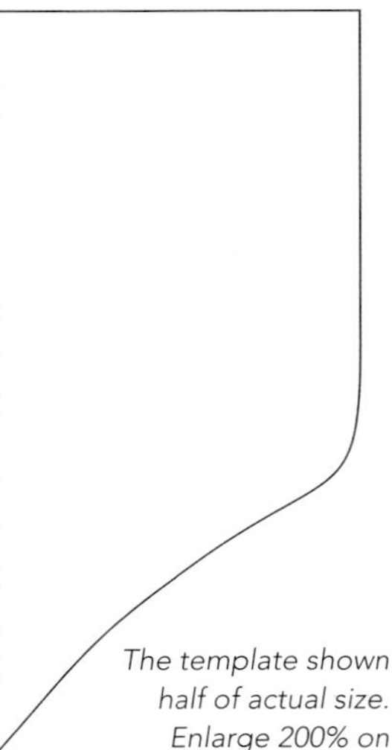

The template shown half of actual size. Enlarge 200% on a photocopier.

5 Using the variegated thread, sew a line of chain stitch (see page 6) along the edge of the folded ribbon, sewing over the flags and tassels as you go. You may need to make a few extra stitches from the back of the ribbon through the ends of the tassel loops to hold them firmly in place. Take out the pins and tacking. Press the ribbon.

I chose four colourways of the same oriental flower-patterned fabric for this bunting. It's a satin fabric, so it works well with the design, but this also means that it isn't the easiest fabric to work with. If you are a novice sewer, use a printed cotton fabric instead.

Snowflake Bunting

Materials:

Paper for templates

For each snowflake: piece of white felt measuring at least 10 x 10cm (4 x 4in)

Sewing thread

1cm (3/8in) white lace and 4cm (1½in) white ric-rac the required length of the bunting, allowing for ties at each end

White pom-pom trim

Tools:

Sewing machine (optional)

Paper scissors

Spray starch

Iron

Fabric marker

Craft knife

Cutting mat

Small, sharp fabric scissors

Hand-sewing needle

Tip: shades of white
The different materials will almost certainly be different shades of white, but this will help to give the bunting a more three-dimensional look.

Instructions:

1 Using hand-sewn running stitches or a straight stitch on the sewing machine, sew the lace along the centre of the length of ric-rac. Turn under and sew the ends of the ric-rac to neaten them.

2 Enlarge the snowflake motifs and cut them out. Folding very accurately and creasing firmly, fold a 10cm (4in) square of paper into eighths. Lay one motif on the resulting triangle and draw round it. Cut out the shapes and open up the paper to produce the snowflake template. Repeat the process with the remaining two motifs.

3 Following the manufacturer's instructions, starch the felt until it is very stiff, starching on one side (which will be the back) only. Lay the templates on the felt and draw out the required number of snowflakes.

4 Cut out the snowflakes, firstly cutting out the central holes with the craft knife on the cutting mat. Use the small, sharp scissors to cut out the edge shape and to trim any stray fluff.

5 Using small stitches, hand-sew the snowflakes to the ric-rac, spacing them evenly. Rotate them so that different elements are at the top to increase the visual variety.

6 Cut individual pom-poms from the trim, unravelling the braid a little so that each pom-pom has a tail. Sew a pom-pom to the ric-rac between each snowflake, stitching through the tail, and another to the top of each snowflake.

The templates shown half of actual size. Enlarge 200% on a photocopier.

This looks seasonally beautiful either as bunting to decorate the house or wrapped around the tree as a contemporary version of a garland. Team it with white baubles and faux snow to create a winter wonderland.

Butterfly Bunting

Materials:

Paper for template

For each butterfly: piece of felt measuring at least 14 x 12cm (5½ x 4¾in)

Selection of sequins in different sizes and colours

Seed beads

Sewing thread

Daisy trimming the required length of the bunting, allowing for ties at each end

Tools:

Paper scissors

Spray starch

Iron

Fabric marker

Fabric scissors

Beading needle

Hand-sewing needle

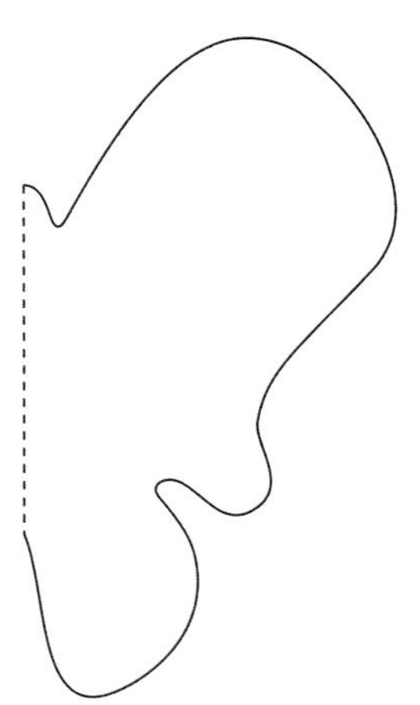

The template shown half of actual size. Enlarge 200% on a photocopier.

Instructions:

1 Enlarge the butterfly motif and cut it out to make a template.

2 Following the manufacturer's instructions, starch the felt until it is very stiff, starching on one side (which will be the back) only. Lay the templates on the felt and draw out the required number of butterflies. Cut out each one.

3 Using the beading needle and sewing thread, decorate each butterfly with sequins. Bring the needle up where you want the sequin to be, slip one or more sequins on to the needle, topped by a seed bead. Skipping the bead, take the needle down through the sequins and fabric. Bring up the needle at the position of the next sequin.

4 Using tiny stab stitches (see page 6), sew the top of each butterfly wing to the back of the daisy trim, spacing the butterflies evenly.

Once the butterflies have been cut out, your children can help with decorating them. These are rather exotic butterflies in vivid colours with sparkling markings. For a more shabby chic species of butterfly, choose a cream or pale teal felt and decorate the wings with small buttons or appliqué spots.

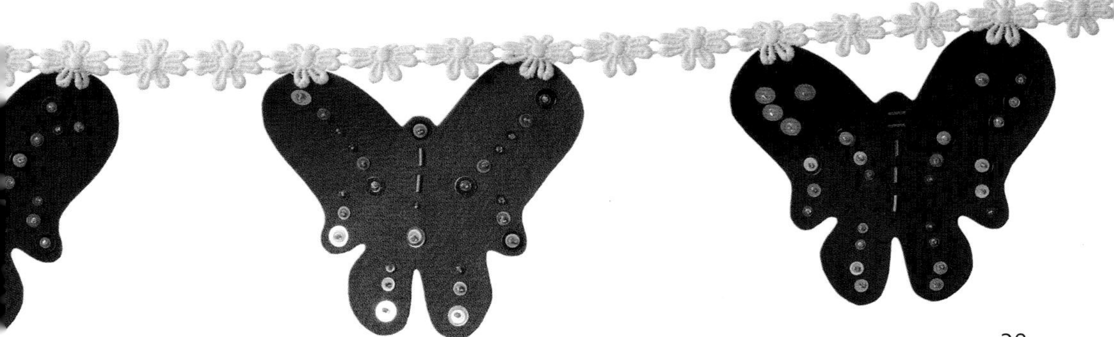

Elegant Bunting

Materials:

Card for template

For each pennant: two pieces of fabric measuring at least 17 x 20cm (6¾ x 8in)

Sewing thread

4cm (1½in) jumbo ric-rac the required length of the bunting, allowing for ties at each end

One small button for each pennant

Tools:

Pencil

Ruler

Paper scissors

Fabric marker

Fabric scissors

Pins

Sewing machine

Iron

Hand-sewing needle

Instructions:

1 On the card draw a triangle 17cm (6¾in) wide across the top and 20cm (8in) from top to tip. Cut this out to make a template. Use the template and fabric marker to draw as many pennants as you need on to the fabric. Cut out each one and pin them together in pairs, right sides together, matching all edges.

2 Set the sewing machine to a medium straight stitch. Taking a 1cm (3/8in) seam allowance, machine-sew down both sloping sides of each pennant (see page 7), leaving the straight top edge open.

3 Trim the seam allowances and clip the point of each pennant (see page 7). Turn each pennant right side out and press flat. You will find the end of a knitting needle useful for turning out the point, but be careful not to push the needle right through the fabric.

4 Set the sewing machine to a medium zigzag stitch. Sew across the top of each pennant to stiffen the edge and prevent it from fraying.

5 Pin each pennant to the back of the ric-rac, spacing them evenly. Using small oversewing stitches through the back of the ric-rac (make sure the stitches don't show on the front), hand-sew each pennant in position.

6 Sew a small button to the tip of each pennant.

7 Turn under and sew down the ends of the ric-rac to neaten them.

Tip: calculating the width of your pennants
The precise width of your pennants may depend on the ric-rac you use. I wanted my pennants to sit neatly on the scallops of my ric-rac, so I measured the required distance and made that the width, adding 1cm (3/8in) all around for seams.

Choosing a variety of fabrics within one colour palette makes for a sophisticated bunting that looks elegant in any room. Jumbo ric-rac in a toning colour adds an original touch.

Flower Bunting

Materials:

Scraps of lace and ruffle trimmings

Lace flower motifs

Sewing thread

One decorative button for each flower

Seed beads

2.5cm (1in) velvet ribbon the required length of the bunting, allowing for ties at each end

Scraps of felt

Craft glue

Tools:

Fabric scissors

Hand-sewing needle

Pins

Fabric marker

Pinking shears

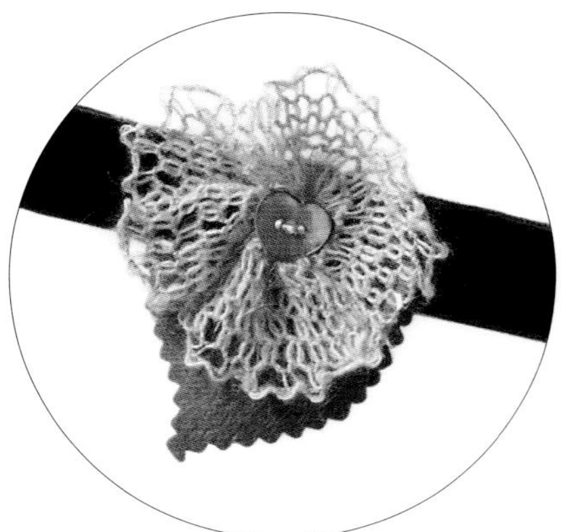

Instructions:

1 Cut a short length of trimming; from 5cm (2in) to 8cm ($3\frac{1}{8}$in) will usually be enough, depending on the trimming. Using doubled thread, sew a line of small running stitches along the lower edge. Pull up the stitches tightly and fan out the trimming to form a circle. Join the ends of the circle with tiny stitches. Make as many flowers as needed in this way. Individual lace motifs can be used as they are.

2 Position the flowers on the ribbon. When you are happy with the arrangement, mark the position of each flower with a pin. Remove the flowers, keeping them in order so that you know which one goes on each marked point.

3 Sew a button into the centre of each flower, at the same time sewing the flower to the ribbon. Make two stitches through the holes in the button, then come up through one hole, thread on two or three seed beads and go down through the other hole.

4 Lay a piece of felt behind a flower, so that the top edge of the felt lies about 5mm (¼in) below the top edge of the ribbon. Using the fabric marker, draw a leaf shape on the felt protruding below the flower. Cut out the leaf shape with pinking shears, extending the cuts to the top of the felt. Repeat to make a leaf for each flower.

5 Apply a strip of craft glue to the top of each leaf in turn and glue it to the back of the ribbon, behind a flower.

This is such pretty bunting that can be made from all sorts of delicious scraps of trimming and ribbon. Choose a limited colour palette, as I have, or go wild and create a multicoloured garland using as many shades as possible.

Groovy Bunting

Materials:

For each pennant: two pieces of printed fabric measuring at least 17 x 20cm (6¾ x 8in)

Sewing thread

Strip of straight-grain fabric (or several joined strips) measuring 5cm (2in) by the required length of the bunting, allowing for ties at each end

Tools:

Fabric marker

Ruler

Fabric scissors

Pins

Sewing machine

Iron

3cm (1¼in) bias tape maker

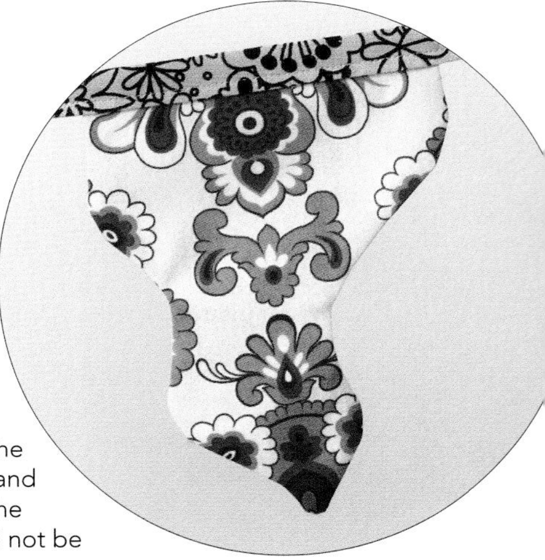

Instructions:

1 Pin pieces of fabric together, right sides together, for the front and back of each pennant. Using the fabric marker and ruler, draw pennants of different sizes and shapes on to the fabrics. The top edge must be straight and curves should not be too tight. Cut out the pennants.

2 Set the sewing machine to a medium straight stitch. Taking a 1cm (3/8in) seam allowance, machine-sew down both long sides of each pennant (see page 7), leaving the straight top edge open.

3 Trim and clip the seam allowances (see page 7). Turn each pennant right side out and press it flat.

4 Following the manufacturer's instructions, thread the strip of straight-grain fabric through the tape maker and iron the folds into tape as they emerge. Press the tape in half lengthways.

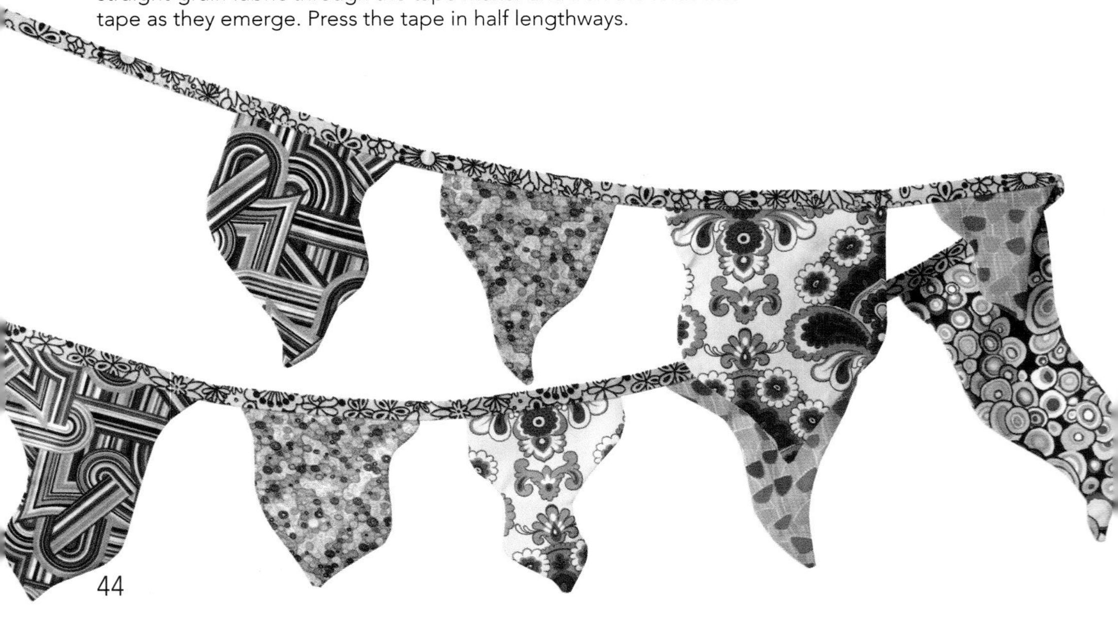

5 Slip the top edge of each pennant into the tape, spacing the pennants evenly. Pin each one in place. Turn under and pin the ends of the tape to neaten them.

6 Set the sewing machine to a medium straight stitch. Starting at one end of the tape, machine along it close to the open edge, sewing over each pennant and taking out the pins as you go. Press the bunting.

Choose mismatched prints for this vibrant bunting that will bring 70s retro style to the most minimal room. Draw the pennants freehand, making sure the curves are not too tight or they will be tricky to sew.

Lavender Baby Bunting

Materials:

Card for template

For each pennant: two pieces of gingham fabric measuring at least 14 x 15cm (5½ x 6in)

Sewing thread

2.5cm (1in) gingham ribbon the required length of the bunting, allowing for ties at each end

Dried lavender

Tools:

Pencil

Ruler

Paper scissors

Fabric marker

Fabric scissors

Pins

Sewing machine

Iron

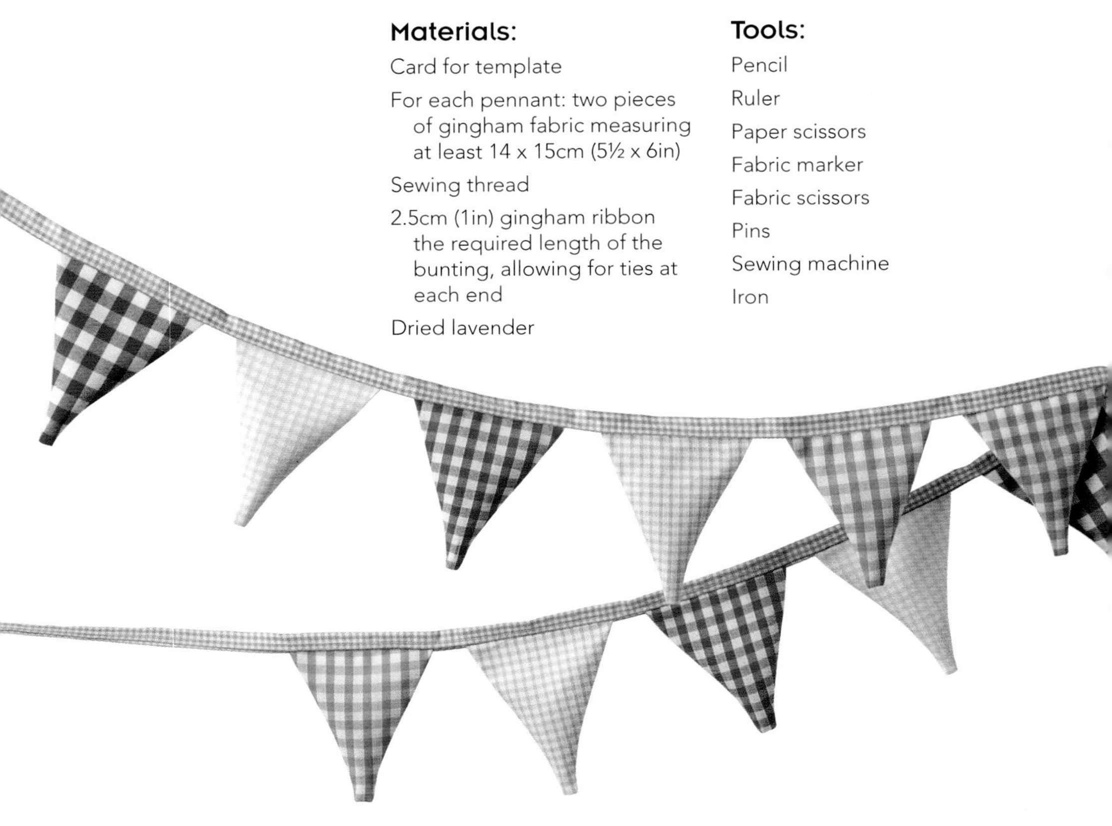

Instructions:

1 On the card draw a triangle 13cm (5in) wide across the top and 14.5cm (5¾in) from top to tip. Draw a line straight across the triangle 1cm (3/8in) up from the tip and cut the tip off. Cut this shape out to make a template. Use the template and fabric marker to draw as many pennants as you need on to the fabric. Cut each one out and pin them together in pairs, right sides together, matching all the edges.

2 Set the sewing machine to a medium straight stitch. Taking a 1cm (3/8in) seam allowance, machine-sew down both sloping sides of each pennant and across the bottom, leaving the straight top edge open.

3 Trim and clip the seam allowances (see page 7). Turn each pennant right side out and press flat.

4 Working on one pennant at a time, tip a small amount of dried lavender into the pennant. Set the sewing machine to a medium zigzag stitch and sew across the top.

5 Fold the ribbon lengthways, so that one edge slightly overlaps the other, the overlapping side will be the front. Press the fold. Slip the top edge of each pennant into the folded ribbon, spacing the pennants evenly. Pin each one in place. Turn under and pin the ends of the ribbon to neaten them.

6 Set the sewing machine to a medium straight stitch. Starting at one end of the ribbon, machine along it close to the open edge, sewing over each pennant and taking out the pins as you go. Press the ribbon.

The pennants of this cute gingham bunting contain lavender to keep the nursery smelling sweet and promote restful sleep. Rubbing the pennants will release more scent and you can refresh it with a little lavender oil.

Acknowledgements

Kate would like to thank the team at Search Press, including Roz Dace for the serendipitous telephone call that resulted in this book, Alison Shaw for her editorial support, Paul Bricknell and Debbie Patterson for taking the lovely photographs and Marrianne Mercer for designing the pages. Thanks, as always, to Philip for the food.

Publisher's Note

If you would like more information about sewing and textiles, try *Sew Scandinavian* by Nadja Knab-Leers & Heike Roland, Search Press, 2010 or *Stylish Sewing* by Laura Wilhelm, Search Press, 2010.

You are invited to visit the author's website www.katehaxell.co.uk